STANDARDS-BASED

SOCIAL STUDIES

ACTIVITIES WITH RUBRICS

Highly Motivating, Literacy-Rich Activities that Reinforce Important
Social Studies Content and Help Students Show What They Know

by Kevin Morris

New York ☆ Toronto ☆ London ☆ Auckland ☆ Sydney   **Teaching**
Mexico City ☆ New Delhi ☆ Hong Kong ☆ Buenos Aires   *Resources*

Acknowledgments

To my parents, who have supported me every step of the way, through college, and everything else!

I would also like to acknowledge the tremendous teaching talents I have encountered along the way—their ideas and passions inspire me to be a better teacher.

Scholastic Inc. grants teachers permission to photocopy the reproducible pages from this book for classroom use. No other part of this publication may be reproduced in whole or in part, or stored in a retrieval system, or transmitted in any form or by any means, electronic, mechanical, photocopying, recording, or otherwise, without written permission of the publisher. For information regarding permission, write to Scholastic Inc., 557 Broadway, New York, NY 10012.

Cover design by Jason Robinson
Interior design by Kelli Thompson
Illustrations by Dave Clegg

ISBN-13: 978-0-439-51783-6
ISBN-10: 0-439-51783-4
Copyright © 2006 by Kevin Morris
All rights reserved.
Printed in the U.S.A.

1 2 3 4 5 6 7 8 9 10   31   15 14 13 12 11 10 09 08 07 06

Table of Contents

Introduction

Enrich your social studies curriculum with this collection of highly innovative projects and games. *Standards-Based Social Studies Activities With Rubrics* features ten learning-rich, small-group projects plus three whole-class games that your students are sure to find appealing. The activities are designed to support your regular curriculum while engaging students in meaningful, academically sound instruction.

This book focuses on the "big ideas" of social studies, with activities that encourage students to make connections throughout history and enable them to see how people and events are interdependent. While some of the projects are specific to particular topics, such as the Declaration of Independence (page 31) or westward expansion (page 35), many are more generalized and can be used with any previously studied unit or even with several units at the same time. The games are perfect for whole-class review, and you can also adapt them for use with other topics. Each activity in this book meets curriculum standards for both

social studies and U.S. history. The standards listed in each activity come from the National Council for the Social Studies (NCSS) and from the Mid-continent Research for Education and Learning's (McREL) Historical Understanding and United States History standards.

Each project includes the following:

Overview – a summary of the activity and its purpose

Standards – for social studies and history, taken from the National Council for the Social Studies and the Mid-continent Research for Education and Learning

Time Frame – approximately how much time you need to allot for each activity. This is based on my own classroom experience, so you may have to adjust the time periods according to your students' levels.

What to Do – easy ways to introduce the activity and get students started in their work

Extra! – variations and/or extensions, management tips, or additional suggestions for implementing the activity into your classroom

Grading Rubric – reproducible grading sheet to help students get a clear understanding of your expectations and how their project will be graded (see "Information and Suggestions About Using Rubrics," page 6)

Student Page – reproducible step-by-step instructions on what students need to do to complete the project. Vocabulary Connection Quilts (page 18) and History-Making Dinner Party (page 39) also include additional reproducible templates for students to use.

I've used all the activities in this book in my classroom, and they are favorites of my students. These activities support all learners; students of varying levels can be successful with each lesson shared. My students have consistently received high scores on state and county standardized testing for social studies.

Information and Suggestions About Using Rubrics

The rubrics I have included have been reworked and refined over my many years of teaching. The ones that you'll find in this book are the most useful that I have found. I have been using them successfully in my classroom for quite some time now. I offer these rubrics to you, but you may find that you need to make changes to better suit your students.

The first thing you might notice about my rubrics is the language. I have taught grades 4 and 6, and I've used these rubrics at both levels without changing the language. I have found that if I spend time with students discussing the language of the rubric, the words and phrases become regular vocabulary.

My students know what the words "above average," "superior," and "unique" mean. We discuss these assessment words regularly. They understand how to provide "original perspectives" because we discuss what doing so means. They know how they can earn a 4 instead of a 3. They grasp that a 3, and even a 2, is a good score, and they can be proud of earning that score. But once I've handed back the rubric, we can sit down together and brainstorm how they might do even better next time. The most important advice I have regarding these rubrics is to discuss them with your students.

Distribute copies of the rubric to students before they start working on an activity. This will help them understand the goals of the activity and how they will ultimately be graded. The criteria on the rubric will not be difficult for students to understand if you discuss them clearly in class.

Even if a student scores a total of 8 (out of 16 possible points) on a rubric, I consider that to be a positive project. There is certainly room for improvement, and I encourage you to discuss scoring with students. Ask them to write or tell you what they could have done to earn 3s and 4s. Invite their parents to do the same. However, in my classroom I have students redo a project if they score a total of 5 or below. I feel that if you explain to a student that his or her work needs improvement, you should give the student a chance to improve it. Once a student has submitted a revised project, I average the original 5 or below with the new score. In my opinion this is a fair way to assess the student's achievement.

In addition, I explain to my students that just because they complete all the required elements, they may not necessarily receive superior marks. I have my students imagine how they would feel if they had to look at 25 or 30 of the same projects. They often moan and groan, and many state how boring that would be. I use this understanding to help stress to them the importance of being unique and original. I ask them to think about what they can do to make their work stand out from the others. Overall scores of "Acceptable" and "Above average" are the most common in my classroom. Students beam when they receive a "Superior" rating because they understand that they have challenged themselves and truly gone above and beyond what was expected of them.

I share these rubrics (and my general style of rubrics) with parents at Back-to-School Night. I explain that scores of "Acceptable" and "Above average" are positive results and should be celebrated. I always encourage parents to discuss with their child what he or she can do to make the next project even better.

If you plan to use rubrics in your classroom on a regular basis, I encourage you to take similar steps and make their language and their use common understanding with your students and parents. Doing so helps create an open and comfortable classroom environment. Enjoy!

Year-Round Journal ★★★★★★★★★★★★★★★★★★★★★★★★★

Overview

In this yearlong activity, students keep a written journal in which they reflect on and write responses to prompts pertaining to key concepts from various units of study. They then trade their written responses with other students for review. After a student reads a classmate's response, he or she will comment on the response.

Standards

HISTORICAL PERSPECTIVE

✓ Understand the broadly defined eras of historical events
✓ Know how to view the past in terms of the norms and values of the time
✓ Understand that specific ideas had an impact on history
✓ Understand that specific decisions and events had an impact on history

SOCIAL STUDIES

✓ Demonstrate an understanding that different scholars may describe the same event or situation in different ways but must provide reasons or evidence for their views
✓ Identify and use key concepts such as chronology, causality, change, conflict, and complexity to explain, analyze, and show connections among patterns of historical change and continuity

Time Frame

☆ About 15 minutes to introduce the prompt and discuss the rubric and student direction sheets.
☆ About 30 to 40 minutes after sharing the prompt for students to answer the prompt effectively. (You might want to have additional assignments on hand for students who finish early.)
☆ About 20 to 30 minutes for students to exchange journals, read their classmates' response, and then write their own response to the answer.

What to Do

Provide each student with about 30 sheets of notebook paper and a manila folder. To create their journal, have students staple the notebook paper into the right-hand side of the folder's interior. Distribute copies of the direction sheets (pages 12–13) and have students staple them to the left-hand side of the folder's interior.

Encourage students to decorate their folder throughout the year. The pictures on the cover should reflect themes and concepts they've learned from various units.

My county provides teachers with "essential questions" that our students need to know. For example, what were the major causes of the Revolutionary War? I use these questions as prompts for my students. Whether you use county-issued questions or create your own questions,

(continued)

keep them open-ended. The prompts should encourage students to reflect on the "big ideas" of the unit and be very broad in nature. I usually use the log only once or twice in each unit. Following are examples of "big idea" prompts:

☆ Describe the relationships between the colonists and the Native Americans throughout English colonization.

☆ How did the ideas of government differ between the colonists and Parliament?

☆ Describe challenges that the United States faced during the Reconstruction period following the Civil War.

☆ What were some motivations and hardships for individuals moving west in the United States?

Encourage students to provide a variety of answers, offer observations, as well as give opinions and facts. Remind students to refer to the direction sheets when answering the prompt.

At the end of the period, I collect students' journals and review responses and score them based on the grading rubric (page 10). The following day (or within the week), I pass out the logs but do not give them back to the owner. Instead, I give them to different students. Using the direction sheets as a guide, students respond to their classmates' answers. Students receive two grades—one for their response to the prompt and another for their response to another student's response (see page 11).

Extra!

☆ Use the prompts to review a unit. Students should have prior knowledge for this activity to be effective.

☆ This activity works well as early morning work. I place the journals on students' desks in the morning and they write their responses when they come in. It also works as a center for language arts instruction. Using this as a center during language arts alleviates 25 to 30 students turning in their journal at the same time and helps with assessment.

☆ With these journals, students can make year-round connections to important themes. Students often have one or two written responses to prompts from every unit studied, plus dialogue from their peers that provides them with other people's perspectives. They also illustrate the cover of their journal throughout the year. By the end of the year, they have a detailed journal reviewing what they've learned throughout the entire year.

☆ Grading and assessing can become somewhat tedious. Consider using one prompt per unit and allow a week to assess all the responses.

Grading Rubric

Name: _____

★ ★ ★ ★ **Year-Round Journal (Writer) Assessment** ★ ★ ★ ★

SCORE	CRITERION
1　2　3　4	Student stated the "big idea" of the prompt.
1　2　3　4	Student supported the "big idea" with specific information and examples.
1　2　3　4	Student gave opinions about the "big idea."
1　2　3　4	Student provided observations and wonderings about the "big idea."

TOTAL:_____/16

✂ -

Grading Rubric

Name: _____

★ ★ ★ ★ **Year-Round Journal (Writer) Assessment** ★ ★ ★ ★

SCORE	CRITERION
1　2　3　4	Student stated the "big idea" of the prompt.
1　2　3　4	Student supported the "big idea" with specific information and examples.
1　2　3　4	Student gave opinions about the "big idea."
1　2　3　4	Student provided observations and wonderings about the "big idea."

TOTAL:_____/16

Name: _____

★ ★ ★ Year-Round Journal (Responder) Assessment ★ ★ ★

SCORE	CRITERION
1 2 3 4	Student agreed or disagreed with the writer's response.
1 2 3 4	Student added other supporting examples for the prompt that the writer did not state.
1 2 3 4	Student provided feedback.
1 2 3 4	Student provided own opinions, observations, or wonderings about the writer's response.

TOTAL:_____/16

- -

Grading Rubric

Name: _____

★ ★ ★ Year-Round Journal (Responder) Assessment ★ ★ ★

SCORE	CRITERION
1 2 3 4	Student agreed or disagreed with the writer's response.
1 2 3 4	Student added other supporting examples for the prompt that the writer did not state.
1 2 3 4	Student provided feedback.
1 2 3 4	Student provided own opinions, observations, or wonderings about the writer's response.

TOTAL:_____/16

Name: _____ Date: _____

My Journal of Big Ideas

★ ★

(Objective)

Keep a journal of important concepts you've learned throughout the year. Share your response with a classmate to gain insight from their response in return.

(Directions and Expectations)

1. You will receive a question or a writing prompt about a recent unit of study.

2. Answer the question in your journal, following the directions below (see "First Responder"). Be sure to include all the required information.

3. After answering the question, switch journals with another student and read his or her response to the same question. Write your own response to your partner's answer. Be sure to include all of the required information in your response (see "Second Responder").

4. You will be scored on your answer to the question as well as your written response to your partner's answer.

FIRST RESPONDER

★ What is the "big idea" of the prompt? State it.

★ Support the big idea with specific information and examples from your social studies notes, textbook, and class discussions.

★ Give your opinions, observations, and wonderings. Start your sentences with:
- "I think . . ."
- "I wonder . . ."
- "I didn't agree . . ."
- "Wow, I never knew . . ."

My Journal of Big Ideas
(continued)

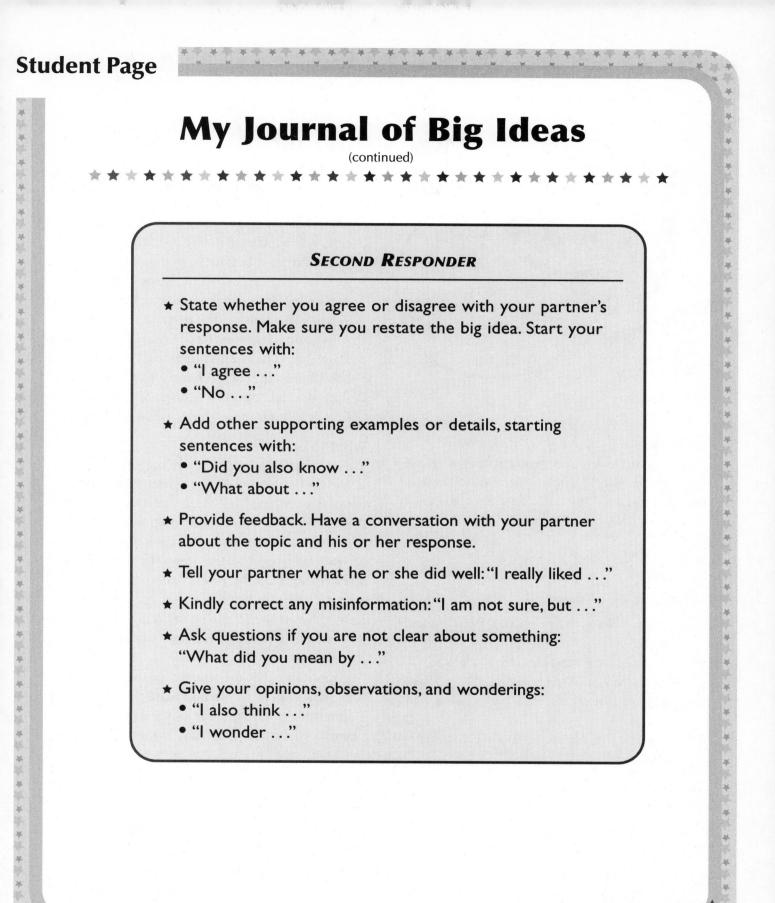

SECOND RESPONDER

★ State whether you agree or disagree with your partner's response. Make sure you restate the big idea. Start your sentences with:
  • "I agree . . ."
  • "No . . ."

★ Add other supporting examples or details, starting sentences with:
  • "Did you also know . . ."
  • "What about . . ."

★ Provide feedback. Have a conversation with your partner about the topic and his or her response.

★ Tell your partner what he or she did well: "I really liked . . ."

★ Kindly correct any misinformation: "I am not sure, but . . ."

★ Ask questions if you are not clear about something: "What did you mean by . . ."

★ Give your opinions, observations, and wonderings:
  • "I also think . . ."
  • "I wonder . . ."

13

History's Greatest Hits CD ★★★★★★★★★★★★★★★★★

Overview

As a wrap-up to a unit of study, students create a musical CD with 10 track titles that reflect what they learned from the unit. Students also design and create their own CD case.

Standards

HISTORICAL PERSPECTIVE

✓ Understand the broadly defined eras of historical events

✓ Know how to view the past in terms of the norms and values of the time

✓ Understand that specific ideas had an impact on history

✓ Understand that specific decisions and events had an impact on history

SOCIAL STUDIES

✓ Identify and describe selected historical periods and patterns of change within and across cultures

Time Frame

☆ A 45- to 60-minute period to introduce the project, discuss the rubric and student direction sheet, brainstorm song titles together, show previous student examples, and allow students to individually start brainstorming their own song titles.

☆ About 15 to 20 minutes of the next two class periods for students to continue generating song titles, brainstorming a possible album title, and sketching their cover. Circulate the class during this time so you can get a clear idea of what each student is working on. This can be helpful in your assessment later on.

☆ A week to complete the rest of the project at home and to turn in the CD case. The finished case should have an attractive CD cover with the album's title and the track titles.

☆ Part of a class period for the class to share their CDs within groups of four or five students.

What to Do

This project is great for reviewing key concepts at the end of a unit. To get my students excited about the project, I tell them that some "bigwigs" from New York want to turn this time period of history into a musical. (Usually the boys are not overjoyed by this news, but once they start working on the project they really get into it.) I tell students that they have to come up with titles for all the songs. They don't have to write the lyrics to the songs, but the titles are important.

Emphasize that the song titles should reflect what students have learned from the unit. Remind them to include important people, places, events, and vocabulary in their song titles. You may want to brainstorm about four or five song titles as a whole class to help students get started.

For example, these song titles would be appropriate for the conclusion of a Civil War unit:

☆ "Where Did Our Rights Go?" (to reflect the Southern state's point of view)

☆ "The Sounds of Sumter" (to denote the beginning of the Civil War)

(continued)

☆ "Brother vs. Brother" (to indicate that families were pitted against each other during the war)

I don't require a written explanation of why students chose their song titles, but I tell them to be prepared to explain their choices to the class. Encourage students to refer to their textbook, social studies notebook, and class notes when thinking about their song titles. I usually give students a set of page numbers from the textbook to help them, and we go through notes and old activities to help them generate ideas.

In addition to writing song titles, students also create a title for their CD that reflects something they learned in that time period. They also design the CD-case album cover.

Extra!

☆ You may want to encourage students to write the lyrics to one or more of their songs for extra credit or to perform their song on the project due date. Some of your more technical students may actually want to create a CD; I always tell my students to go for it. I have had students produce a CD with them singing the lyrics to their songs. These are very neat.

☆ Depending on your student population, you may have to supply CD jewel cases. These can be purchased inexpensively at any electronics store. I usually encourage students to use CD cases that they have at home.

Name: _____

★ ★ ★ ★ ★ ★ ★ ★ **History CD Assessment** ★ ★ ★ ★ ★ ★ ★ ★

SCORE	CRITERION
1　2　3　4	Student created track titles that reflect key concepts learned in the unit of study.
1　2　3　4	Student created track titles that reflect important events, significant individuals, and key vocabulary in the unit of study.
1　2　3　4	Student designed an attractive, eye-catching CD case.
1　2　3　4	Student titled the CD to reflect what was learned in the unit of study.

TOTAL: _____ /16

- -

Grading Rubric

Name: _____

★ ★ ★ ★ ★ ★ ★ ★ **History CD Assessment** ★ ★ ★ ★ ★ ★ ★ ★

SCORE	CRITERION
1　2　3　4	Student created track titles that reflect key concepts learned in the unit of study.
1　2　3　4	Student created track titles that reflect important events, significant individuals, and key vocabulary in the unit of study.
1　2　3　4	Student designed an attractive, eye-catching CD case.
1　2　3　4	Student titled the CD to reflect what was learned in the unit of study.

TOTAL: _____ /16

Name: _____ Date: _____

History's Greatest Hits CD

★ ★

(Objective)

Imagine that you are producing a musical about the historical period that you just studied. What kinds of songs do you think should be in the musical? Create a music CD about this specific time period.

(Directions and Expectations)

1. Produce a music CD with songs about a specific time period:
   * Create 10 different song titles that reflect what you learned about the time period. The titles should clearly indicate key concepts, important people, significant events, and related vocabulary. (For example, say you were studying the early English settlements in America. A possible song title might be "Lumber, Lumber Everywhere," suggesting that the English wanted to get more raw materials from the New World and that colonists got their lumber from all the forests.)
   * You do not have to write the lyrics to each song, although you may do so for extra credit.

2. Design a CD album cover:
   * If possible, use an empty CD case from home. (If you can't find an empty CD case, use construction paper instead.)
   * Design an attractive, eye-catching album cover for the CD.
   * Make an insert for the case and list the song titles inside.

3. Come up with a title for your CD. The title should reflect what you learned from the unit of study.

(Extra)

* Review the rubric to make sure you've completed the work on which you will be assessed.

* If you would like to perform one of your songs for the class, talk to your teacher beforehand.

⭐ 17

Vocabulary Connection Quilts ★★★★★★★★★★★★★★★★★

Overview

Using a list of vocabulary words along with names of important people, places, and events from a unit of study, students create "connection quilts" that piece together these key historic concepts. Students working in small groups will engage in meaningful discussions about important concepts in a given unit and discover how the meanings of words fit together in different ways.

Standards

HISTORICAL PERSPECTIVE

✓ Understand the broadly defined eras of historical events

✓ Understand that specific ideas had an impact on history

SOCIAL STUDIES

✓ Demonstrate an understanding that different scholars may describe the same event or situation in different ways but must provide reasons or evidence for their views

✓ Identify and use key concepts such as chronology, causality, change, conflict, and complexity to explain, analyze, and show connections among patterns of historical change and continuity

Essential Skills

✓ Use appropriate sources to gain meaning of essential terms and vocabulary: glossary, dictionary, text, word lists

✓ Recognize and understand an increasing number of social studies terms

Time Frame

☆ A 30-minute class period to introduce the project, share previous students samples, and discuss the rubric and student direction sheet.

☆ A 45- to 60-minute class period for students to work on this activity.

☆ One or two days at home for students to illustrate their connection quilts.

☆ Part of a class period for students to share their connection quilts.

What to Do

Before starting this activity, create a list of important terms as well as names of people, places, and events covered within a unit.

Divide the class into groups of three or four students and give each group a copy of the list and the blank quilt template (page 21). Encourage each group to discuss the various words and look for connections among them. Then have each group choose four words to make a "connection quilt." They should write a paragraph explaining how the words are connected.

For example, say your class is studying early colonial settlements. One group might choose the following words from the list: *export*, *conflict*, *Powhatan*, and *colonists*. The group might explain that the colonists' cash crop was tobacco, which they *exported* for money. This caused *conflict* with the *Powhatan* Indians because the *colonists* used a lot of the Powhatan's land to grow their tobacco.

Encourage each group to create about four or five connection quilts. Each student then takes a "quilt" and illustrates the concept either at home or during individual work time.

After each group has completed their quilts, invite them to present their quilts to the class. Then put the quilts together to make an attractive wall display.

Extra!

☆ This is an excellent way to differentiate instruction for your students. There are no right or wrong answers. If a student can explain a connection between the various terms using appropriate definitions and examples, consider it correct.

☆ Use this activity to review multiple units. Creating lists that cover several units yields very interesting perspectives and results.

Name: _____

★ ★ ★ ★ ★ ★ **Connection Quilts Assessment** ★ ★ ★ ★ ★ ★

SCORE	CRITERION
1 2 3 4	Student made multiple connections to key concepts using important vocabulary words.
1 2 3 4	Student provided unique and original connections between important vocabulary words.
1 2 3 4	Student wrote a clear and easy-to-understand explanation of each connection quilt.
1 2 3 4	Student illustrated the connection quilts vividly.

TOTAL: _____ /16

- -

Grading Rubric

Name: _____

★ ★ ★ ★ ★ ★ **Connection Quilts Assessment** ★ ★ ★ ★ ★ ★

SCORE	CRITERION
1 2 3 4	Student made multiple connections to key concepts using important vocabulary words.
1 2 3 4	Student provided unique and original connections between important vocabulary words.
1 2 3 4	Student wrote a clear and easy-to-understand explanation of each connection quilt.
1 2 3 4	Student illustrated the connection quilts vividly.

TOTAL: _____ /16

Name: _____ Date: _____

Historical Terms Connection Quilts

★ ★

Objective

Using the attached list of vocabulary words and names of people, places, and events, make multiple connections to key concepts covered in our unit of study. Then create and design a "connection quilt" using some of these words.

Directions and Expectations

1. Choose four words from the attached list. Together with your group, discuss how the four words are connected.

2. Create a "connection quilt" using the four words to show how they are interconnected. Use the attached template for your quilt. Then write a paragraph explaining how the four words fit together.

3. Repeat steps 1 and 2 to create a total of four or five quilts. Each connection quilt should cover different concepts within the unit of study.

4. Give each person in your group a quilt to design and illustrate. The illustration should reinforce the written explanation.

5. Be ready to present your quilts to the class.

Due date: _____

Name: _____ **Date:** _____

Quilt Template

Design your Historical Terms Connection Quilt on this template.

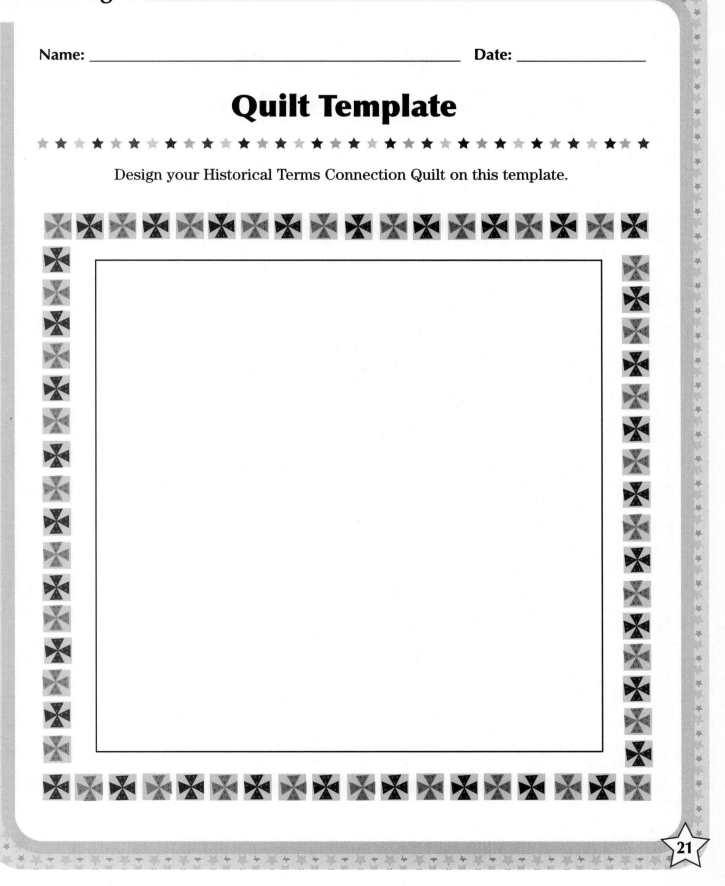

21

Due date: _____

Instant Messenger Buddy List ★ ★ ★ ★ ★ ★ ★ ★ ★ ★ ★ ★ ★ ★ ★

Overview

Students create screen names for important historical individuals based on each individual's accomplishments. Students also design and illustrate icons to represent the individuals. After creating their "buddy list," students choose two individuals to have an instant-message (IM) conversation that shows an understanding of historical perspective.

Standards

HISTORICAL PERSPECTIVE

✓ Understand that specific individuals and the values those individuals held had an impact on history

SOCIAL STUDIES

✓ Demonstrate an understanding of concepts such as role, status, and social class in describing the interactions of individuals and social groups

✓ Develop critical sensitivities such as empathy and skepticism regarding attitudes, values, and behaviors of people in different historical contexts

✓ Identify and describe the influence of perception, attitudes, values, and beliefs on personal identity

Time Frame

☆ Two 45- to 60-minute class periods to introduce the activity, discuss the rubric and student direction sheet, and have students create their screen names and sketch their icons.

☆ Another 45- to 60-minute period (usually in language arts) to allow students to write their draft for their IM conversation.

☆ About three or four days at home for students to make their work presentable (e.g., correct mistakes, add details to icons) and add any final touches.

What to Do

Before starting this activity, generate a list of notable people your class has studied to date. I introduce this activity by talking about my screen name with students. I ask them if they think my screen name makes sense and why and how it represents me. (My student population has easy access to computers and many have their own screen names. I usually invite them to share their screen names and encourage the class to discuss how a student's screen name depicts that student.)

Next, ask students: "What if Thomas Jefferson had a screen name?" or "If Susan B. Anthony was typing an instant message, what might she say?" My students often giggle about this, but they

(continued)

quickly start brainstorming ideas. Choose two or three notable individuals you've already discussed during the year, and together as a class, decide on a screen name and an icon for one individual.

Distribute your list of important historical people to students. Have them choose up to 10 people from the list and make up a screen name and icon for each person. The screen name should be no longer than 15 characters. For example, Thomas Paine's screen name could be MAKCENTS ("make sense"). He wrote *Common Sense* and helped persuade people to fight for independence.

After students have created their screen names and icons, invite them to choose two individuals to have an instant-messaging (IM) conversation. Their conversation should be appropriate and reflect historical perspective. Encourage students to include as many facts from history as they can.

Extra!

☆ You might want to do a smaller-scale version of this activity at the end of each unit and track all the important people you study throughout the year. I know some teachers who keep a large buddy list on display in their room all year long. This activity also serves as a great year-end review.

☆ Some students have created "chat rooms" and had more than two of their "buddies" conduct a conversation about a specific topic. This makes a great higher-level thinking extension.

Name: _____

★ ★ ★ **Instant-Messenger Buddy List Assessment** ★ ★ ★

SCORE	CRITERION
1 2 3 4	Student created a screen name that reflects an important accomplishment of an individual.
1 2 3 4	Student created a screen name that shows unique and original thinking.
1 2 3 4	Student wrote an instant-message conversation that is meaningful and includes specific historic examples and perspectives.
1 2 3 4	Student illustrated an appropriate eye-catching icon.

TOTAL:_____/16

✂ --

Grading Rubric

Name: _____

★ ★ ★ **Instant-Messenger Buddy List Assessment** ★ ★ ★

SCORE	CRITERION
1 2 3 4	Student created a screen name that reflects an important accomplishment of an individual.
1 2 3 4	Student created a screen name that shows unique and original thinking.
1 2 3 4	Student wrote an instant-message conversation that is meaningful and includes specific historic examples and perspectives.
1 2 3 4	Student illustrated an appropriate eye-catching icon.

TOTAL:_____/16

Name: _____ Date: _____

Our Buddies in History

★ ☆ ★ ☆ ★ ☆ ★ ☆ ★ ☆ ★ ☆ ★ ☆ ★ ☆ ★ ☆ ★ ☆ ★ ☆ ★ ☆ ★ ☆ ★

Objective

Whom in history would you include in your instant-messenger buddy list? Choose up to 10 important people that you've studied so far this year and decide what screen name would best represent each one.

Directions and Expectations

1. Create a buddy list of 10 notable people and a screen name for each person:
   ★ Each screen name should reflect the accomplishments of the individual. (For example, WRK4FD could be an appropriate screen name for John Smith. He implemented the "work for food" rule in the Jamestown colony to get more people to work.)
   ★ The screen names should show unique and original thinking. It should not be more than 15 letters.

2. Design and illustrate an appropriate icon (the little image next to a screen name on a buddy list) for each screen name. The icon should reflect the importance of the individual.

3. Transcribe at least one instant-messaging conversation between two individuals. The conversation should be about important historical events and include each person's historical perspective. Pretend that you are the two individuals typing the instant-message conversation.

Standards-Based Social Studies Activities with Rubrics • Scholastic Teaching Resources

Due date: _____

Name: _____ Date: _____

Our Buddies in History

(continued)

★ ★

Reminders

★ Choose people from a variety of time periods to make your instant-messaging conversations much more interesting.

★ Screen names are usually not very long; they're short and to the point. How can you say a lot with only a few letters?

★ Have fun with the icons. What are some cool icons you've seen before?

★ Be sure to include specific facts in your instant-messaging conversation. Double-check all your information to make sure your facts are all correct.

★ Review the rubric to make sure you've effectively completed the work on which you will be assessed.

Due date: _____

The Preamble Project ★ ★ ★ ★ ★ ★ ★ ★ ★ ★ ★ ★ ★ ★ ★ ★ ★ ★

> *We the people of the United States, in order to form a more perfect Union, establish justice, insure domestic tranquility, provide for the common defense, promote the general welfare, and secure the blessings of liberty to ourselves and our posterity, do ordain and establish this Constitution for the United States of America.*
>
> —Preamble to the Constitution of the United States

Overview

Students will make meaningful connections to each line of the Preamble to the Constitution of the United States. They will paraphrase each line of the Preamble, create a visual connection through a poster or mobile, and cite examples of how the Constitution appears in our society's daily life.

Standards

SOCIAL STUDIES

✓ Examine persistent issues involving the rights, roles, and status of the individual in relation to the general welfare

✓ Examine the origins and continuing influence of key ideals of the democratic republican form of government, such as individual human dignity, liberty, justice, equality, and the rule of law

✓ Identify and interpret sources and examples of the rights and responsibilities of citizens

Time Frame

☆ About 15 minutes to introduce the activity and discuss the rubric and student direction sheets.

☆ Two 45- to 60-minute class periods to discuss each part of the Preamble and for students to paraphrase the Preamble and brainstorm examples of how our Constitution appears in our society's everyday life.

☆ One to two weeks to complete the poster or mobile at home.

☆ Part of a class period for students to share their projects.

What to Do

If possible, display a copy of the Preamble on the board. Introduce the Preamble to students and, together, read it aloud. Discuss as a class what students notice about this introduction to the Constitution.

Provide each student with a copy of the Preamble. Have them circle words they don't know and encourage them to use the dictionary and ask one another to find the meanings of words they don't know or understand.

Next, discuss each phrase with the class and brainstorm ideas about what the line means. Challenge students to think of real-life examples of how the meaning of the line is reflected in our country today. For example, the phrase "provide for the common defense" could mean to protect our country, prompting students to talk about the U.S. Army, Navy, or Coast Guard.

Encourage students to rewrite each line of the Preamble in their own words. Then have them create a poster or mobile displaying the information discussed. If they would like to present their information in a different format, encourage them to talk with you and get approval.

Standards-Based Social Studies Activities with Rubrics • Scholastic Teaching Resources

Grading Rubric

Name: _____

★ ★ ★ ★ ★ ★ **Preamble Project Assessment** ★ ★ ★ ★ ★ ★

SCORE	CRITERION
1　2　3　4	Student paraphrased each line of the Preamble.
1　2　3　4	Student created an example for each line that reflected how the ideas in the Preamble appear in present day.
1　2　3　4	Student vividly illustrated each example.
1　2　3　4	Student created a poster, mobile, or other visual that was neat, easy to understand, and attractive.

TOTAL:_____/16

✂ -

Grading Rubric

Name: _____

★ ★ ★ ★ ★ ★ **Preamble Project Assessment** ★ ★ ★ ★ ★ ★

SCORE	CRITERION
1　2　3　4	Student paraphrased each line of the Preamble.
1　2　3　4	Student created an example for each line that reflected how the ideas in the Preamble appear in present day.
1　2　3　4	Student vividly illustrated each example.
1　2　3　4	Student created a poster, mobile, or other visual that was neat, easy to understand, and attractive.

TOTAL:_____/16

Name: _____ Date: _____

Paraphrasing the Preamble

★ ★

Objective

Get to know the Preamble to the Constitution of the
United States by rewriting it in your own words and
creating a Preamble poster or mobile. (Note: If you
want to present the information in another format,
get approval from the teacher.)

Directions and Expectations

1. Paraphrase (put in your own words) each line of
   the Preamble to the Constitution of the United
   States. Each line should be separated as follows:

   We the people of the United States/

   in order to form a more perfect Union/

   establish justice/

   insure domestic tranquility/

   provide for the common defense/

   promote the general welfare/

   and secure the blessings of liberty to ourselves and our posterity/

   do ordain and establish this Constitution for the United States of America.

★ **29**

Paraphrasing the Preamble

(continued)

★ ★

2. Create a poster or mobile to represent the Preamble. Your project should include the following:

★ Each line of the Preamble to the United States Constitution paraphrased (rewritten in your own words).

★ An example of how that line is reflected in our country today.

★ An illustration for each line. You may also use magazine clippings, clip art from the computer, or other type of graphics to illustrate each line.

(Example)

For the line "establish justice," you might say that this means to create courts and make laws for people to follow. An example of this in our country today is the United States Supreme Court. You might illustrate this line with a gavel, judge, or court building.

(Reminders)

★ Include as many examples of each line as you can. The more examples you include, the better!

★ Make sure that your visual is neat, detailed, and easy to follow.

★ Review the rubric to make sure you've effectively completed the work on which you will be assessed.

Due date: _____

The Declaration of Independence Collage ★ ★ ★ ★ ★ ★ ★ ★

Overview

Students will understand the meaning of the words *life*, *liberty*, and *the pursuit of happiness* and gain an appreciation of how the ideals of the Declaration of Independence exist in our government and daily lives. Each student will create a collage on large (9" x 18") poster board with images from magazines, computer clip art, newspapers, and students' own illustrations that reflect the meaning of the words. Students should be prepared to explain orally how the images they chose represent the words.

Standards

SOCIAL STUDIES

✓ Examine persistent issues involving the rights, roles, and status of the individual in relation to the general welfare

✓ Give examples and explain how governments attempt to achieve their stated ideals at home and abroad

✓ Examine the origins and continuing influence of key ideals of the democratic republican form of government, such as individual human dignity, liberty, justice, equality, and the rule of law

✓ Identify and interpret sources and examples of the rights and responsibilities of citizens

U.S. HISTORY

✓ Understand the major ideas in the Declaration of Independence, their sources, and how they became unifying ideas of American democracy (e.g., major terms, why the document was written)

Time Frame

☆ A 30-minute class period to introduce the project, share previous student samples, and discuss the rubric and student direction sheet.

☆ One 45- to 60-minute class period to have students work in groups and brainstorm images for the words.

☆ A week for students to complete the project at home.

☆ Part of a class period for students to share their collages in small groups.

What to Do

After introducing and discussing the Declaration of Independence, focus on the three key terms in the introduction of the document: *life*, *liberty*, and *the pursuit of happiness*. Emphasize to students that these words helped shape our nation. Explain that decisions made by Thomas Jefferson and other writers of the Declaration were based on the ideas behind these words. The shape and face of our government today reflect these words, and certain things in our daily lives are based on the ideas behind these words.

Divide the class into six groups. Assign two groups the word *life*, two groups the word *liberty*, and the last two groups the words *pursuit of happiness*. Provide each group with a dictionary so students can look up the basic definition of their words. Then ask the groups to brainstorm ideas of how their word appears in their daily lives.

Most groups initially need help with this, so we brainstorm a few ideas together. Provide a few examples, such as: "If you have the right to lead a safe life, how is that possible?" Students might respond with police, rules, and laws. "If you have the right to follow your dreams and goals and get a good education, how is that possible?" Students might respond with schools. I often add that state and county governments provide these schools.

After students have generated some good ideas with their group, challenge them to work individually and think of images that represent their words. They will use these images to create their own collages. Make sure you circulate around the class during this time to get a clear idea of what each student is working on. This can be helpful in your assessment later on.

At the end of the project, place students in groups of five or six to share their collage and discuss the images that they chose.

Name: _____

★ ★ ★ ★ **Declaration of Independence Assessment** ★ ★ ★ ★

SCORE	CRITERION
1　2　3　4	Student created a collage with images that reflect the meaning of the words *life*, *liberty*, and *the pursuit of happiness*.
1　2　3　4	Student utilized unique and original perspectives when choosing images.
1　2　3　4	Student created a neat, organized collage; white space was minimal.
1　2　3　4	Student provided clear explanations of how the images they chose represent their own feelings and beliefs about the words.

TOTAL: _____ /16

- -

Grading Rubric

Name: _____

★ ★ ★ ★ **Declaration of Independence Assessment** ★ ★ ★ ★

SCORE	CRITERION
1　2　3　4	Student created a collage with images that reflect the meaning of the words *life*, *liberty*, and *the pursuit of happiness*.
1　2　3　4	Student utilized unique and original perspectives when choosing images.
1　2　3　4	Student created a neat, organized collage; white space was minimal.
1　2　3　4	Student provided clear explanations of how the images they chose represent their own feelings and beliefs about the words.

TOTAL: _____ /16

Standards-Based Social Studies Activities with Rubrics • Scholastic Teaching Resources

Name: _____   Date: _____

Pictures of Independence

★ ☆ ★ ☆ ★ ☆ ★ ☆ ★ ☆ ★ ☆ ★ ☆ ★ ☆ ★ ☆ ★ ☆ ★ ☆ ★

Objective

What do the words *life, liberty, and the pursuit of happiness* mean to you? Create a collage that reflects the meaning of these words and share it with the class. (Note: If you would prefer to make something other than a collage, get approval from the teacher.)

Directions and Expectations

1. Choose images that reflect what the words *life, liberty, and the pursuit of happiness* mean to you and how these words appear in our society today.
   - ★ Create the collage on a 9" x 18" poster board.
   - ★ You may use magazine clippings, computer clip art, and your own illustrations for the collage. Use a variety of images.
   - ★ The words *life, liberty, and the pursuit of happiness* should appear prominently on your collage.

33

Due date: _____

Pictures of Independence

(continued)

★ ★

2. Be prepared to explain how the images that you chose represent the important words from the Declaration of Independence and how they reflect your opinions and beliefs. Here are some questions you might want to consider to help you with your collage:

★ What things are important in your life?

★ What do you consider happiness to be?

★ What does liberty mean to you?

★ How will the United States of America protect these things?

★ How does the United States of America make these things possible for you?

(Examples)

Life – to be able to live in peace and safety

Liberty – to be free from oppression

Pursuit of happiness – to be able to follow your dreams and achieve your goals in life

(Reminders)

★ Make sure you fully understand why you chose each image. You will need to explain this clearly to your teacher and classmates.

★ Fill as much space on the poster board as possible. Don't leave any white space.

★ Review the rubric to make sure you've effectively completed the work on which you will be assessed.

34

Due date: _____

Little Shop on the Prairie ★★★★★★★★★★★★★★★★★★★★★

Overview

This project is a perfect wrap-up to a pioneer/westward-expansion unit. Students will create a store that pioneers would have encountered in their journey west. The decisions students make about the store—including its name and the kinds of things for sale—should reflect their knowledge of the type of people moving west, their motivations for making the move, and the hardships they encountered on their journey.

Standards

SOCIAL STUDIES

✓ Compare similarities and differences in the ways groups, societies, and cultures meet human needs and concerns
✓ Give and explain examples of ways that economic systems structure choices about how goods and services are to be produced and distributed
✓ Describe the role that supply and demand, prices, incentives, and profits play in determining what is produced and distributed in a competitive market system
✓ Explain and illustrate how values and beliefs influence different economic decisions

✓ Use economic concepts to help explain historical and current developments and issues in local, national, or global contexts

U.S. HISTORY

✓ Understand how the industrial revolution, increasing immigration, the rapid expansion of slavery, and the westward movement changed American lives and led to regional tensions
✓ Understand elements of early western migration (e.g., the lure of the West and the reality of life on the frontier; motivations of various settlers; Mormon contributions to the settlement of the West; differences in the settlement of California and Oregon in the late 1840s and 1850s; routes taken by settlers of the Western U.S.; interactions between settlers and Native Americans in the western territories)

Time Frame

☆ A 45- to 60-minute class period to introduce the project and discuss the rubric and student direction sheet.
☆ About 15 minutes during the next two classes for students to draft their ideas.
☆ About two weeks for students to complete the rest of the project at home.
☆ Part of a class period for students to share their projects.

What to Do

Engage students in a discussion about what makes a store successful. In discussions with my class, we often conclude that the best store is one that caters to the widest range of people.

Ask students: "What do you think a store along the Oregon Trail might have sold?" (Some of my students respond: "Bibles because people were religious" or "Spades because people were trying to mine gold.")

Tell students that they are going to create a store located in the West during the pioneer days. Invite them to think of a good store name,

Little Shop on the Prairie ★★★★★★★★★★★★★★★★★★★★★

(continued)

making sure that it reflects something they learned from the unit. With my class, we brainstorm names that would not be good. "The Old West Store," for example, does not reveal any knowledge about the time period. Make sure students understand that vocabulary words and concepts discussed from the unit should appear in the title of their store. Then have students design an eye-catching sign for their store.

Next, discuss the inventory list. Explain to students that their store supplies should appeal to the type of people moving west. The goal is to get as many people as possible to shop there by offering what people want.

Lastly, have students create a slogan for a postcard and a T-shirt that they would sell in their store. Have them think about tourist shops that sell postcards and T-shirts that tout the city they're in. Again, the slogans should reflect something they learned from the unit. For example, a catchy slogan might be: "Oregon—Come on out, there's plenty of room!" This shows an understanding that people were moving west to escape the big city and own their own land. We brainstorm slogans that would not be good and discuss reasons why.

Extra!

☆ Present this project at the conclusion of your pioneer/westward-expansion unit. Students should have a good understanding of the objectives in order to create quality projects that make great connections.

☆ If they're up to it, encourage students to create actual T-shirts with their slogans.

☆ I've had students who gave presentations that were like sales pitches. One student even pretended that she was trying to get investors to invest in her store. Encourage original thinking!

☆ You can turn this project into an excellent wall display. You can potentially get such a variety of final projects—hand-made signs, T-shirts, postcards large and small, unique inventory lists, and so on. It looks great!

Standards-Based Social Studies Activities with Rubrics • Scholastic Teaching Resources

Name: _____

★ ★ ★ ★ Little Shop on the Prairie Assessment ★ ★ ★ ★

SCORE	CRITERION
1 2 3 4	Student met each required element by creating a store name and sign, a supply list, and a slogan for a postcard or T-shirt.
1 2 3 4	Student utilized important concepts learned within the unit of study in all of the required elements.
1 2 3 4	Student displayed unique and original thinking.
1 2 3 4	Student created neat and attractive elements.

TOTAL:_____/16

Grading Rubric

Name: _____

★ ★ ★ ★ Little Shop on the Prairie Assessment ★ ★ ★ ★

SCORE	CRITERION
1 2 3 4	Student met each required element by creating a store name and sign, a supply list, and a slogan for a postcard or T-shirt.
1 2 3 4	Student utilized important concepts learned within the unit of study in all of the required elements.
1 2 3 4	Student displayed unique and original thinking.
1 2 3 4	Student created neat and attractive elements.

TOTAL:_____/16

Name: _____ Date: _____

Old West General Store

★ ★

Objective

Set up shop in the Old West, where pioneers would have stopped by to stock up on goods. What would you name your store? What would you sell?

Directions and Expectations

1. Think of a store name that reflects something you learned in our unit of study. Design and create the sign for your store.

2. Make an inventory list (items that you would have sold at your store) that contains at least 25 items that pioneers would have needed and bought.

3. Create a slogan for a T-shirt or postcard to sell in your store. The slogan should also reflect something important you learned about the westward expansion.

Example

Naming a store "Independence Rock Stop" shows your knowledge about Independence Rock being an important landmark on the Oregon Trail. Pioneers knew that they had to have reached this rock by July and that it marked the halfway point of their journey west. An appropriate slogan could be: "You're halfway there!" Your inventory list could include items for kids because many families moved west, bibles because many people moved for religious reasons, and gold pans because people were hoping to find gold out west.

Reminders

★ Make sure your sign, inventory list, and postcard/T-shirt are vividly illustrated and look neat.

★ Remember, everything you create should be based on historical fact. Double-check all your information!

★ Think: What can you do to make your project stand out? Think about fun things that you can add but are not required.

★ Review the rubric to make sure you've effectively completed the work on which you will be assessed.

Due date: _____

History-Making Dinner Party ★ ★ ★ ★ ★ ★ ★ ★ ★ ★ ★ ★ ★ ★

Overview

This activity makes an engaging end-of-the-year review of everything you have studied in class. Students put together a dinner guest list consisting of eight people from different time periods in history. Based on what they know about each person, students plan a seating chart, putting together people with similar interests and/or backgrounds. They then either write a paragraph explaining what their guests have in common or transcribe a conversation their guests might have.

Standards

HISTORICAL PERSPECTIVE

✓ Understand that specific individuals and the values those individuals held had an impact on history

SOCIAL STUDIES

✓ Demonstrate an understanding of concepts such as role, status, and social class in describing the interactions of individuals and social groups
✓ Develop critical sensitivities such as empathy and skepticism regarding attitudes, values, and behaviors of people in different historical contexts
✓ Identify and describe the influence of perception, attitudes, values, and beliefs on personal identity

Time Frame

☆ About 15 minutes to introduce the activity and discuss the rubric and student direction sheet.
☆ Two or three 45-minute class periods to complete this activity.
☆ Part of a class period for students to share their project.

What to Do

Before starting this activity, generate an extensive list of important individuals from different periods of history that your class has covered. Divide the class into groups of two or three students. (This activity can also be done as an individual project.) Provide students with a blank seating chart (page 42) and the list of possible dinner guests.

Inform students that they will be hosting a dinner party in which they can invite eight people from the list. After selecting their guests, have students decide where and with whom their guests will sit. (At this point, you may want to share with students how you feel when going to a party or get-together and how it helps to seek out people with whom you have something in common, like another teacher perhaps.) Remind students to think about what their guests have in common with one another when planning the seating arrangement. Encourage students to make unique connections and not seat together two individuals who already know each other, such as Patrick Henry and Thomas Jefferson. Insist that students make connections across time periods. For example, Rosa Parks and Abraham Lincoln could have a lively conversation about the importance of racial equality.

After students have filled out their seating chart, have them write at least one paragraph explaining why they grouped certain people together or transcribing a conversation between two or more people at the dining table. Then invite students to illustrate and color their dinner-table seating charts.

Extra!

☆ I have shared this idea with colleagues and in turn have heard some interesting variations on this activity. For example, students might take on the role of certain historical persons and, during a history lunch party, "perform" the dialogue they wrote. Other teachers have created large wall displays of the dinner table with life-size portraits of the individuals and students' written explanations of the guests' connections.

Standards-Based Social Studies Activities With Rubrics • Scholastic Teaching Resources

Name: _____

★ ★ ★ ★ **History-Making Dinner Party Assessment** ★ ★ ★ ★

SCORE	CRITERION
1 2 3 4	Student made meaningful connections between key historical figures and their accomplishments.
1 2 3 4	Student provided relevant examples to support connections between individuals.
1 2 3 4	Student provided unique and original perspectives with connections.
1 2 3 4	Student illustrated and designed dinner table vividly.

TOTAL: _____/16

✂ -

Grading Rubric

Name: _____

★ ★ ★ ★ **History-Making Dinner Party Assessment** ★ ★ ★ ★

SCORE	CRITERION
1 2 3 4	Student made meaningful connections between key historical figures and their accomplishments.
1 2 3 4	Student provided relevant examples to support connections between individuals.
1 2 3 4	Student provided unique and original perspectives with connections.
1 2 3 4	Student illustrated and designed dinner table vividly.

TOTAL: _____/16

Name: _____ Date: _____

Guess Who's Coming to Our History Dinner Party?

★ ★

Objective

You are hosting a very important dinner party with some of the most significant persons from different times in history. Whom would you invite? What would your guests talk about? Plan a seating chart to ensure that everyone sits next to someone with whom he or she has something in common.

Directions and Expectations

1. Invite eight people from the attached guest list and decide where each guest will sit:
  ★ Seat each guest next to a person with whom he or she has something in common. The people you put next to each other should be able to discuss historical events as well as their accomplishments. (Although each guest will be sitting between two people, he or she could have a conversation with only one of the people. As an extra challenge, however, try to find things in common with both neighbors.)
  ★ Complete the attached seating chart.

2. Write a paragraph explaining what each grouping of people have in common or what they might talk about. You may want to write an actual conversation between two or more individuals.

3. Decorate the dinner table, using bright colors to illustrate your table.

Reminders

★ Try to come up with unique connections. Thomas Jefferson and Benjamin Franklin, for example, would not be unique since they already know each other. However, Benjamin Franklin and Thomas Edison, who lived in different time periods, could discuss their inventions.

★ Double-check all the facts you include in your paragraph, making sure that all your information is correct.

★ Review the rubric to make sure you've completed the work on which you will be assessed.

★ 41

Due date: _____

Name: _____ Date: _____

History Dinner Seating Chart

★ ★

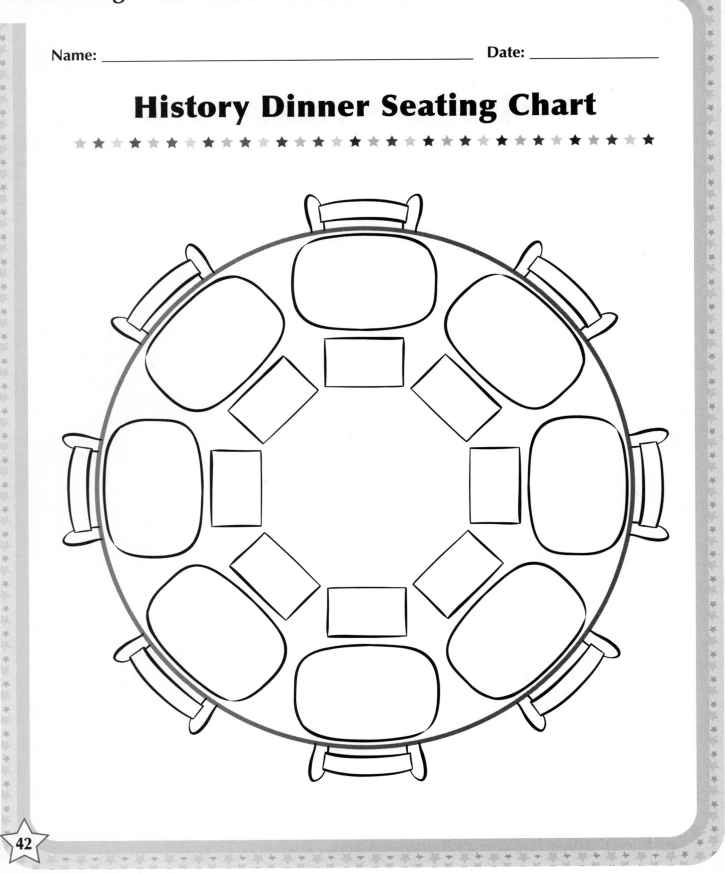

Standards-Based Social Studies Activities with Rubrics • Scholastic Teaching Resources

Due date: _____

States of the Union ★

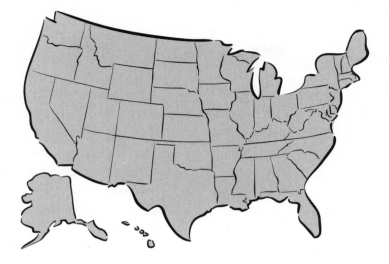

Overview

Students hone their research skills to find specific information about a particular state. Then they incorporate their report on a large piece of poster board that they cut and design to resemble the shape of their state. At the end of the project, you can use students' posters to rebuild a map of the United States and to provide students with information about other states.

Standards

SOCIAL STUDIES

✓ Elaborate mental maps of locales, regions, and the world that demonstrate understanding of relative location, direction, size, and shape

✓ Create, interpret, use, and distinguish various representations of the earth, such as maps, globes, and photographs

✓ Estimate distance, calculate scale, and distinguish other geographic relationships such as population density and spatial distribution patterns

✓ Locate and describe varying landforms and geographic features, such as mountains, plateaus, islands, rain forests, deserts, and oceans, and explain their relationships within the ecosystem

✓ Describe physical system changes such as seasons, climate and weather, and the water cycle and identify geographic patterns associated with them

✓ Describe how people create places that reflect cultural values and ideals as they build neighborhoods, parks, shopping centers, and the like

✓ Describe ways that historical events have been influenced by, and have influenced, physical and human geographic factors in local, regional, national, and global settings

Time Frame

☆ About 15 minutes to introduce the activity and discuss the rubric and student direction sheet.

☆ Three or four 45- to 60-minute language arts class periods for students to conduct research. Allow students who do not finish during this time period to continue their research during independent-work time.

☆ About two weeks for students to complete the poster at home. I usually allow class time for students to cut their poster board in the shape of the state. This can be pretty tricky for many students.

☆ Part of a class period for students to share their projects.

What to Do

You might want to assign students a state randomly. I usually have students pick state names from a hat. (When I started this activity,

States of the Union ★

(continued)

I was team teaching and had two classes of 25 students, so every state was accounted for. If possible, try to figure out a way to have all 50 states accounted for.)

Distribute copies of the student sheets (pages 46–47), which includes a list of questions to guide students' research about their state. You might want to discuss this activity with your librarian beforehand so he or she can pull out necessary resources for students. Encourage students to use multiple resources and to do all their research in class. This project meets researching skills standards, and this is valuable time to spend with students in class.

When students have completed their research, explain the requirements for their poster. Students need to cut their poster in the shape of their state and incorporate all the information they've researched on the poster.

On the due date, divide the class into groups of about five to seven students and have them share their projects with one another.

Extra!

☆ If you can account for each state, you might want to have students go outside and try to assemble the United States using their posters. Of course, to pull this off, students' state posters need to be close to the same scale. In any case, this gives students a good idea of where states are located. I have done this before as a whole class—it worked better when I had a teacher's aide take students out in small groups of five to seven to rebuild the country using the posters.

☆ Use the posters to create a scavenger hunt for students. For example, clues could include: "This state is known for peanuts," or "What state has a grizzly bear on its flag?" Lay out all the posters (or do this activity after the map is created) and have students work in pairs to conduct the hunt.

☆ If your school has a large supply of colored poster board, you might want to use colors to represent the regions. For example, students with mid-Atlantic states could have green poster boards.

Standards-Based Social Studies Activities with Rubrics • Scholastic Teaching Resources

Name: _____

★ ★ ★ ★ ★ **States of the Union Assessment** ★ ★ ★ ★ ★

SCORE	CRITERION
1 2 3 4	Student provided a variety of specific information about his or her state.
1 2 3 4	Student answered all required questions.
1 2 3 4	Student created an attractive and detailed poster displaying all the information he or she found. The poster is in the shape of the assigned state.
1 2 3 4	Student delivered a clear and easy-to-understand oral presentation sharing all the information he or she learned about the state.

TOTAL:_____/16

✂ -

Grading Rubric

Name: _____

★ ★ ★ ★ ★ **States of the Union Assessment** ★ ★ ★ ★ ★

SCORE	CRITERION
1 2 3 4	Student provided a variety of specific information about his or her state.
1 2 3 4	Student answered all required questions.
1 2 3 4	Student created an attractive and detailed poster displaying all the information he or she found. The poster is in the shape of the assigned state.
1 2 3 4	Student delivered a clear and easy-to-understand oral presentation sharing all the information he or she learned about the state.

TOTAL:_____/16

Name: _____ Date: _____

The Great State Search

★ ★

(Objective)

Find out as much information as you can about a particular state using various resources from the library or your classroom. (You will either be assigned the state or pick it out of a hat.)

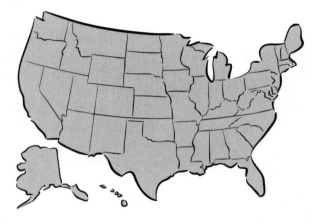

(Directions and Expectations)

1. Use multiple resources in your classroom or library to answer the following questions:
   ★ In what region of the United States is your state located?
   ★ What is your state's capital?
   ★ What are some major cities in your state? Describe some of these cities.
   ★ What landforms make up your state?
   ★ What is the general climate of your state?
   ★ What is the estimated population of your state?
   ★ What type of work do people do in your state?
   ★ What are some famous events that take/took place in your state?
   ★ What are your state's major exports?
   ★ Briefly describe your state's history.
   ★ What other information is important to know about your state?

2. Take a large piece of poster board and cut it into the shape of your state. Use this poster board to display the information you've uncovered.
   ★ Use the whole poster board — do not cut out a smaller version of the state. For example, if you have New Mexico, you would not have to cut the poster board at all!
   ★ Design your poster so that it is attractive and shows your creativity.

Standards-Based Social Studies Activities with Rubrics • Scholastic Teaching Resources   **Due date:** _____

The Great State Search

(continued)

★ ★

- ★ Make sure the information you put on your poster is neat and easy to read. Even more important, make sure the information is correct! Your poster will be used by other students to learn about your state, and we will be constructing a large map of the United States using everyone's poster.

- ★ Your state's name and flag should appear on your poster. You might want to use letter stencils to write the state name.

Reminders

- ★ Did you answer every question? Does the answer to every question appear on your poster?

- ★ Think about how you can make your state poster stand out. What extra things can you include to make it unique and different?

- ★ Review the rubric to make sure you've effectively completed the work on which you will be assessed.

47

Due date: _____

Classroom Regions ★ ★ ★ ★ ★ ★ ★ ★ ★ ★ ★ ★ ★ ★ ★ ★ ★ ★

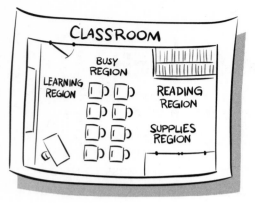

Overview

This activity serves as a great introduction to your regions unit. Students identify and name four to six regions that best describe the classroom and explain why the separation makes sense. They will then draw a map of the classroom, illustrating the different regions. Students can then apply this knowledge when discussing the regions of the United States or of your state.

Standards

SOCIAL STUDIES

✓ Elaborate mental maps of locales, regions, and the world that demonstrate understanding of relative location, direction, size, and shape

✓ Locate and describe varying landforms and geographic features, such as mountains, plateaus, islands, rain forests, deserts, and oceans, and explain their relationships within the ecosystem

✓ Examine, interpret, and analyze physical and cultural patterns and their interactions, such as land use, settlement patterns, cultural transmission of customs and ideas, and ecosystem changes

Time Frame

☆ About 15 minutes to introduce the activity and discuss the rubric and student direction sheet.

☆ Two 45- to 60-minute class periods for students to complete this activity.

☆ Allow time for students to finish the map during individual-work time or at home.

What to Do

Whether you teach regions of the United States or of your state, you might want to introduce the topic by asking students to define the word *region*.

Next, ask students to look around the classroom and see if they can identify some regions in the classroom. Brainstorm a few possible ideas. Encourage students to explain why the region they chose makes sense. For example, one of my students named one area of the classroom the "teacher region." In my classroom, all the materials I need are in one area—I have a wardrobe full of supplies, a teacher desk, and a bookshelf or two of manuals and reference materials. This also feeds into the chalkboard area. The student explained that students usually don't go to this area of the room. There are no materials for them to use, and since I am often at the chalkboard, the students see that as "my area."

As students decide on the classroom's regions, have them think about the following: What does the region look like (as in "landforms" of the region)? What is the "land" of the region mostly used for? What "type" of people use the region? How are the regions different from one another?

Pair up students and have them identify four to six regions, name them, write a short description of each region, and then create a map. Then invite students to share their maps and choices of regions.

Extra!

☆ In Virginia, where I teach, our fourth graders have to know our five regions. I find this activity really helps students understand the reasons for different regions within our state. This unit of study becomes much more meaningful for them when they are learning the differences in our state. I often refer to students' maps when discussing differences in the regions of our state.

☆ Students' maps make a great classroom display.

Name: _____

★ ★ ★ ★ ★ ★ **Classroom Region Assessment** ★ ★ ★ ★ ★ ★

SCORE	CRITERION
1 2 3 4	Student effectively divided the classroom into four to six regions.
1 2 3 4	Student wrote explanations with specific information for creating the regions.
1 2 3 4	Student wrote a clear description of each region.
1 2 3 4	Student vividly illustrated a map showing the regions of the classroom.

TOTAL:_____/16

✂ -

Grading Rubric

Name: _____

★ ★ ★ ★ ★ ★ **Classroom Region Assessment** ★ ★ ★ ★ ★ ★

SCORE	CRITERION
1 2 3 4	Student effectively divided the classroom into four to six regions.
1 2 3 4	Student wrote explanations with specific information for creating the regions.
1 2 3 4	Student wrote a clear description of each region.
1 2 3 4	Student vividly illustrated a map showing the regions of the classroom.

TOTAL:_____/16

Name: _____ Date: _____

Region Reformation

★ ★

Objective

Identify four to six regions in your classroom and create a map that shows
each region.

Directions and Expectations

1. Look around the classroom and think about how you might divide it into four to
   six regions. Base your decision on what each area of the classroom is used for.
   Think: What do things in that area have in common? What is the "land" of the
   area like?

2. After you have identified the regions, name each region and write a paragraph
   explaining what makes that area of the classroom a specific region.

3. Create a map of the classroom showing the regions you've created. Make sure the
   name of each region appears on the map. The map should accurately reflect how
   the classroom is organized.

Example

You might call the classroom library the "Reading Region." You might explain that it
contains beanbag chairs, couches, and several bins of books for students to read.
The "land" is made up of pillows, couches, and rugs.

Reminders

★ Your map should be neat and easy to read
  and contain no more than six regions.

★ Your explanation should clearly describe
  each region of the classroom.

★ Review the rubric to make sure you've
  effectively completed the work on which
  you will be assessed.

Standards-Based Social Studies Activities with Rubrics • Scholastic Teaching Resources

Due date: _____

Introducing the Games

I've developed three very successful games that I play with my students every year. We use these often throughout the year, and I find that my students never get tired of them. These games are not to be used as teaching tools but rather to help students review and process important concepts, vocabulary, people, and events. These games are much more successful when they are used for review. The more knowledgeable students are about a unit, the more effective these games are and the more engaged students will be in the activity. Use these games at the conclusion of every unit and at the end of the year as a wrap-up to a year of study.

I deliberately did not include any sample lists of people, vocabulary, or events. Every state, county, and district develop their own curriculum that focuses on different terms, people, and events. In addition, state, county, and district requirements of essential knowledge for students vary greatly. I felt that including lists of people, terms, or events might limit the potential of these games. I leave it to you, the teacher, to create the content most appropriate for your students. Enjoy!

Standards-Based Social Studies Activities with Rubrics • Scholastic Teaching Resources

Ready, Set, DRAW!

OVERVIEW

This game is similar to the popular games "Win, Lose or Draw" and "Pictionary®." Students make visual and symbolic connections to important vocabulary, key events, and significant people studied within a specific unit.

Note: ESOL (English Speakers of Other Languages) and special-education students tend to do very well at these games. Using symbols and pictures is an excellent way for these students to express themselves.

YOU'LL NEED

★ large tablets of blank white paper, white construction paper, or a whiteboard

★ large markers (dry-erase markers if you're using a whiteboard)

★ category game cards for different categories (teacher created)

★ stopwatch or timer

BEFORE YOU START

For the category game cards, create Vocabulary cards (about 15 to 20), Event cards (covering major events discussed in the unit), and People cards (featuring important individuals studied within the unit).

Ready, Set, DRAW!

(continued)

Note: On page 55, you'll find blank templates for the game cards. However, you might consider creating the game cards using PowerPoint. This way, not only will you have cards for the game, but you will also have a ready-made PowerPoint presentation you can use for future classes. Print the cards and laminate for use.

HOW TO PLAY

1. Divide the class into four or five teams. Having several teams ensures all students are actively engaged in the activity.

2. Teams take turns choosing a category and drawing what is on the clue card. The goal is for each team to solve two clues from each category, for a total of six cards.

3. At their turn, a team assigns a "drawer" to draw the clue. (Team members rotate as the drawer at each turn.) The drawer looks at the clue card then gets 60 seconds to sketch the clue. For example, say the vocabulary word is *export*. The drawer might sketch a picture of the United States, an arrow coming out of the country to another country, and a dollar sign. (Drawers may not use words, letters, or numbers. However, symbols, such as a cross or dollar sign, are allowed.)

4. The drawer's team tries to guess the clue, calling out guesses until the 60 seconds is over.

★ If the team guesses correctly, they keep the clue card and play moves to the next team.

★ If the team guesses incorrectly, the next team gets a chance to guess the clue. If they guess correctly, they get to keep the clue card.

Standards-Based Social Studies Activities with Rubrics • Scholastic Teaching Resources

Ready, Set, DRAW!

(continued)

5. Teams track their own scores by counting how many clue cards they have. The team with the most cards at the end of the game wins.

VARIATIONS

★ If you're playing this game to review multiple units, each unit could serve as a category.

★ Even if you're reviewing just a single unit, you could still adapt the categories to fit your unit. For example, if you're studying the Revolutionary War, two categories might be "loyalist words" and "patriot words."

★ I have had "all-play rounds" before, where one student draws in front of the entire class and any student in the room can guess the clue. The first student to make a correct guess takes the clue card for his or her team. That team then gets to draw next. (This means some teams would get skipped.)

★ Another variation of the "all-play round" is to have all the teams' drawers sketch the same clue at the same time. Again, the team that correctly guesses first gets the clue card and takes control of the drawing. Students enjoy this tremendously, however, be prepared for a very rambunctious classroom!

★ It's also fun to have a "teacher round," where the teacher draws a clue for each team and the students have to guess the answer.

Games

Ready, Set, DRAW! CATEGORY CARDS

Ready, Set, DRAW! Category: _____ Word: _____	**Ready, Set, DRAW!** Category: _____ Word: _____	**Ready, Set, DRAW!** Category: _____ Word: _____
Ready, Set, DRAW! Category: _____ Word: _____	**Ready, Set, DRAW!** Category: _____ Word: _____	**Ready, Set, DRAW!** Category: _____ Word: _____
Ready, Set, DRAW! Category: _____ Word: _____	**Ready, Set, DRAW!** Category: _____ Word: _____	**Ready, Set, DRAW!** Category: _____ Word: _____

55

Charade and Shout!

OVERVIEW

This game, perfect for an end-of-the-year review, helps students associate key words or phrases with a historical individual, as well as connect some kinesthetic movements to the same individual. Students hear several clues repeated throughout the game, reinforcing their knowledge of the individual.

YOU'LL NEED

★ Famous Persons game cards (teacher created)

★ stopwatch or timer

BEFORE YOU START

Create up to 25 game cards that feature notable persons from your unit of study. You might want to download images of each person from the Internet and paste them on the cards. This helps students make visual connections to the individuals during play. **Note:** On page 60, you'll find blank templates for the game cards. However, you might consider creating the game cards using PowerPoint. This way, not only will you have cards for the game, but you will also have a ready-made PowerPoint presentation you can use for future classes. Print the cards and laminate for use.

HOW TO PLAY

This game is played in three rounds with multiple teams. Divide the class into four or five teams. Having several teams ensures all students are actively engaged in the activity.

Charade and Shout!

(continued)

ROUND 1

1. The first team takes a deck of the Famous Persons cards. One person on the team will call out the clues to his or her team. In this first round, the team MAY NOT PASS. The clue giver can say anything except "rhymes with" or "starts with the letter . . ." For example, say a student has Thomas Jefferson. She could say: "I was a president . . . I bought the Louisiana Territory . . . I wrote the Declaration of Independence . . ." etc.

2. Each team gets 45 seconds to guess as many persons as they can. The team gets to keep the cards they guessed correctly. When time is up, shuffle the remaining cards and pass the deck to the next team.

3. Teams continue taking turns until all cards have been used. Teams get one point for each Famous Persons card they keep. Add up the scores.

4. Collect all the clue cards, shuffle the deck, and continue play into Round 2. (Teams use the same deck for all three rounds.)

ROUND 2

1. In this round, a clue giver may say only TWO WORDS for his or her team to guess the person. For example, for Thomas Jefferson, a clue giver might say "Declare Independence" or "Louisiana Purchase." Remember, if the clue giver says more than two words for each Famous Person card, his or her team must pass.

2. If the clue giver's team cannot guess the person or if the clue giver can't think of a good clue, he or she may pass and move on to the next card. There is no limit to how many times a clue giver passes.

Standards-Based Social Studies Activities with Rubrics • Scholastic Teaching Resources

Charade and Shout!

(continued)

3. Allow 45 seconds for each team to guess as many persons as they can. The team gets to keep the cards they guessed correctly. When time is up, shuffle the remaining cards and pass the deck to the next team.

4. Teams continue taking turns until all cards have been used. Teams get one point for each Famous Persons card they keep. Tally up the scores and add them to the teams' previous scores.

5. Collect all the clue cards, shuffle the deck, and continue play into Round 3.

ROUND 3

1. This round is ONLY CHARADES. No noise, no sound! To mime Thomas Jefferson, for example, a clue giver might point to England on a map and make a "no" sign (props are okay). The clue giver could also act like she's sitting at a desk writing a document, or act like he's buying something from someone, pointing to Louisiana on a map. Remember, it's all charades.

2. If the clue giver's team cannot guess the person, he or she may pass and move on to the next card.

3. Allow 60 seconds for each team to guess as many persons as they can. The team gets to keep the cards they guessed correctly. When time is up, shuffle the remaining cards and pass the deck to the next team.

4. Teams continue taking turns until all cards have been used. Teams get one point for each Famous Persons card they keep. Tally up the scores and add them to the teams' previous scores.

5. The team that has the most points after three rounds wins the game.

Standards-Based Social Studies Activities with Rubrics • Scholastic Teaching Resources

Charade and Shout!

(continued)

NOTES

★ Play all three rounds, if possible. This really helps students connect to important accomplishments of individuals in a variety of ways.

★ Sometimes a clue giver might get really stumped and have difficulty thinking of clues. I allow "teacher help" in each round. A clue giver can ask me for help one time in a round when he or she is giving clues.

★ Encourage students to pay close attention to the important people in the deck. Memorizing the people is very important!

★ I play this game about two or three times a year. It's perfect for reviewing multiple units. Then we play the game one last time to review the entire year. Students love this game!

59

Charade and Shout! FAMOUS PERSONS CARDS

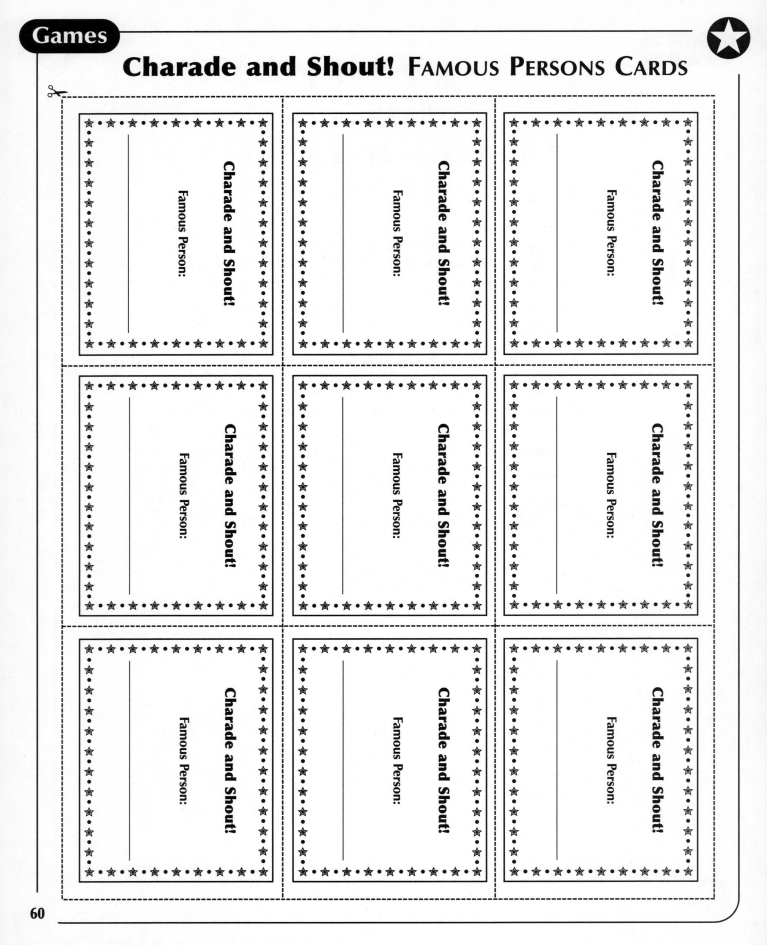

Charade and Shout!

Famous Person:

Charade and Shout!

Famous Person:

Charade and Shout!

Famous Person:

Charade and Shout!

Famous Person:

Charade and Shout!

Famous Person:

Charade and Shout!

Famous Person:

Charade and Shout!

Famous Person:

Charade and Shout!

Famous Person:

Charade and Shout!

Famous Person:

Credit!

OVERVIEW

This game is very similar to "Scattergories®," in which players try to come up with unique responses to general categories. Students work in small teams to show their depth of knowledge about important vocabulary, people, places, and events.

YOU'LL NEED

★ category game cards (teacher created)
★ notebook paper
★ pens and/or pencils

BEFORE YOU START

Create category game cards for students to respond to, using the blank card templates on page 64. Possible categories could include:

★ Reasons for English exploration
★ Places explorers ventured to
★ Causes of the Civil War
★ Something George Washington might have said
★ Important Civil War battles
★ Benjamin Franklin's inventions
★ Important amendments to the Constitution
★ Something you would have encountered moving out west
★ One of the 13 original colonies
★ Important documents in history
★ What a Native American might have thought about settlers

Credit!

(continued)

HOW TO PLAY

1. Divide the class into four or five teams. Having several teams keeps all students actively engaged in the activity.

2. Announce a category for students to provide a response. For example, you might say something like "Events that led to the Revolutionary War." Of course, there are several events from which students can choose. Encourage students to discuss possible answers with their group and then decide on their response. Give students enough time to discuss the answer. (I usually don't put a time limit on group discussion. Instead, I play it by ear and call time when I feel it's appropriate.)

3. When you feel students have had enough time to discuss their answer, move on to the next category. Continue calling out categories until you've gone through about seven to ten categories.

4. Next, invite students to read their answers out loud for each category.

★ Teams with unique answers (only their group has that particular answer) get "credit" for their response and score a point.

★ Cross off any responses that are the same as another team's response. None of the teams with the same answers gets credit.

★ If a team answers incorrectly (as decided by you), that team does not get credit. However, allow teams to defend questionable responses. Remember, the teacher is the ultimate judge; your opinion on responses is final!

5. The team with the most credits (points) wins.

Credit!

(continued)

WHY THIS GAME WORKS!

Think about all the events leading to the Revolutionary War. There were quite a few! The most popular answers would probably be the French and Indian War or the Stamp Act. Team members have to challenge themselves to think of answers besides the obvious, prompting a discussion about all of the other events that led to the Revolutionary War. This helps students recall information that might have been forgotten otherwise.

Also, students get to hear other groups' answers that they might not have thought about themselves. This can be a great learning opportunity in which the whole class can discuss important terminology or significant persons, places, or events.

VARIATION

Challenge students to come up with as many answers as possible to score points. For example, instead of trying to come up with a unique answer, players list all the causes of the Revolutionary War. Each correct answer earns a point, whether or not other teams have the same answer.

Credit! CATEGORY CARDS

Credit!

Category:

Credit!

Category:

Credit!

Category:

Credit!

Category:

Credit!

Category:

Credit!

Category:

Credit!

Category:

Credit!

Category:

Credit!

Category:

Standards-Based Social Studies Activities with Rubrics • Scholastic Teaching Resources